EVERYTHING STARTS FROM PRAYER

"Saint Teresa was one of the great spiritual servants of our era, whose simple wisdom expressed untold depths of devotion. In this treasury of her thoughts on prayer, she offers the world another blessing."

—President Jimmy Carter, author of *Living Faith*

"Using this book on prayer, please remember that Saint Teresa always prayed with her actions, her life. Mind, speech, and body in perfect oneness, that is the solid ground of authentic meditation. The moment you start praying that way, peace, love, and transformation begin to take place, within yourself and around you. You do not have to wait for the result in the future. Saint Teresa says: 'the fruit of prayer is faith, love, service, and peace. All of these take place in the present moment.' Enjoy praying with her."

—Thich Nhat Hanh, author of *Living Buddha, Living Christ*

"Mother Teresa's life was a living prayer. Her words remind us of her connection with God and how all of us can reach Him as she did."

—Marianne Williamson, author of *Illuminated Prayers*

"With the publication of *Everything Starts from Prayer*, Mother Teresa continues to bless us from beyond the grave. These kernels of truth from the nun in Calcutta provide food for the soul. Her messages, though short on words, are deep in wisdom and spiritual insight, and hold meaning for people of all faiths."

—Most Reverend Anthony M. Pilla, Bishop of Cleveland, Past
President, National Conference of Catholic Bishops

"Dr. Stern deserves to be congratulated for *Everything Starts from Prayer*, an inspiring book intended to foster the spiritual life of people of all faiths or none. We hope and pray that many readers will find it an invitation to pray."

—Father Edward Le Joly, Mother Teresa's spiritual advisor

"Dr. Stern's editorial hand is sure and judicious; the selection of material reveals the mystical realization behind Mother Teresa's powerful encomium to prayer in an all-inclusive sense. Thus, the passages are not only spiritually inspiring (as one would, of course, expect), but intellectually compelling as well. Well done."

—Lou Nordstrom, American Zen Teacher,
White Plum lineage

"Dr. Stern has very sensitively and carefully given us the essence of a truly spiritual person, and in the process helped make prayer in our own lives more rewarding."

—Rabbi Jack Bemporad, Director, The Center for Interreligious
Understanding at Ramapo College

"Mother Teresa is a holy mother to us all. She always has been an inspiration and reminder to me of what love can do in the world. She is the epitome of a Bodhisattva, the altruistic enlightenment-activist serving those suffering in this world."

—Lama Surya Das, Tibetan Buddhist master
and author of *Awakening the Buddha Within*

"How do we start praying? Anthony Stern gives us a great gift. In this magnificent collection of Mother Teresa's words, we are shown how to cultivate our inner lives and bring forth the prayers that live within us."

—Prof. Susannah Heschel, author of
Abraham Geiger and the Jewish Jesus

"These beautiful prayer instructions transcend all boundaries of time and space. Here Mother Teresa is a universal figure reaching out from soul-to-soul to all those who pray or long to pray. May her words reach many and open hearts."

—Rabbi Arthur Green, co-editor of *Your Word is Fire:
The Hasidic Masters on Contemplative Prayer*

"This book's contents and its title say it all. Whatever you are looking for starts with prayer. Hopefully you will read and learn that true prayer is not about personal desires, needs or religions. Mother Teresa is a role model for each of us. Pray we may became what she was, and heal the world by using prayer to lead us on the path to spirituality and God."

—Bernie Siegel, M.D., author of *Love, Medicine and Miracles*

EVERYTHING
STARTS FROM
PRAYER

Mother Teresa's
MEDITATIONS ON SPIRITUAL LIFE
FOR PEOPLE OF ALL FAITHS

———————

SELECTED AND ARRANGED BY
ANTHONY STERN, M.D.

FOREWORD BY
REV. DIANE BERKE

HOMILY OF HIS HOLINESS POPE FRANCIS
FOR MOTHER TERESA'S CANONIZATION

Monkfish Book Publishing Company
Rhinebeck, New York

First edition: 1998
Second edition: 2009
Third edition: 2018

Paperback ISBN 978-1-958972-14-4
eBook ISBN 978-1-958972-15-1

Library of Congress Cataloging-in-Publication Data

Names: Teresa, Mother, Saint, 1910-1997, author. | Stern, Anthony, other.
Title: Everything starts from prayer : Mother Teresa's meditations on
   spiritual life for people of all faiths / Selected an arranged by
   Anthony Stern, M.D. ; foreword by Rev.. D iane Berke ; Homily of his
   holiness Pope Francis for Mother Teresa's canonization.
Description: Rhinebeck, New York : Monkfish Book Publishing Company, 2023.
   | Previously published: Ashland : White Cloud Press, 2018. | Includes
   bibliographical references.
Identifiers: LCCN 2023023778 (print) | LCCN 2023023779 (ebook) | ISBN
   9781958972144 (paperback) | ISBN 9781958972151 (ebook)
Subjects: LCSH: Prayer--Meditations.
Classification: LCC BL560 .T47 2023 (print) | LCC BL560 (ebook) | DDC
   204/.33--dc23/eng20230926
LC record available at https://lccn.loc.gov/2023023778
LC ebook record available at https://lccn.loc.gov/2023023779

Book and cover design by Colin Rolfe

Monkfish Book Publishing Company
22 East Market Street, Suite 304
Rhinebeck, New York 12572
(845) 876-4861
monkfishpublishing.com

CONTENTS

Foreword to the Fourth Edition *by Rev. Diane Berke*   ix
Introduction *by Anthony Stern, M.D.*   xii

1. The Need to Pray   1
2. Starting with Silence   11
3. Like a Little Child   21
4. Opening Your Heart   43
5. Ending in Silence   59
6. The Fruit of Prayer   65

Homily of His Holiness Pope Francis
for Mother Teresa's Canonization   93
Introduction to the Second Edition: Mother Teresa's
Faith and Doubt *by Anthony Stern, M.D.*   97
Foreword to the First Edition *by Larry Dossey, M.D.*   103
Retreat Resources   109
Further Reading   111
Sources & Acknowledgments   125
About the Authors   131

FOREWORD TO THE FOURTH EDITION

At the height of the AIDS crisis—sometime in the 1980s or 90s—Mother Teresa (now St. Teresa of Calcutta) was interviewed during a trip she made to New York City to minister to the people who were ravaged by and dying from the virus. When asked to comment about the material affluence available to so many in the West compared to the extreme poverty of those she served in Calcutta, she pointed out that there was a different kind of suffering here. While most people in the West were not suffering the pain of *physical hunger and lack,* she said, many were, in fact, suffering the pain of *spiritual hunger and lack.* Many were starving for human connection, for kindness, for *love.*

Her words had a deep impact on me. Having grown up in a family that deeply valued generosity and giving, I was in the habit of always carrying some change or a few dollars that I could give to the people on the street who would ask. But in reading Mother Teresa's interview, I realized that giving material help in the form of money was not enough. By itself, it did not address an even deeper need that was unspoken but perhaps even more important. I made a promise to myself that, from then on, I would also give love: a moment of connection, a moment of eye contact, a wish or blessing for the sufferer's well-being and peace. Even when I had no money to give, I could still offer love through a moment of care, attention, recognition, and acknowledgment of their humanity. Somehow those simple moments of human connection always left me feeling that I was the one who had received a blessing and gift.

In *Everything Starts from Prayer*, Mother Teresa tells us that the purpose of our lives—the "greater aim," as she calls it—is to love and be loved. And she tells us that our ability to love begins, and grows and deepens, in prayer. The activity of prayer, in its myriad expressions and forms, can be found in every religion and spiritual tradition, and the need for prayer seems to be inherent in the human heart.

Many of us grew up thinking of prayer as simply talking to God—sometimes sharing our joys and gratitude with God, but more often telling God our troubles and fears and asking God for what we want and believe will make us happy. Pouring ourselves out to God this way in prayer, letting ourselves *come as we are* into God's presence and sharing with total honesty what we feel and what we believe we need—is often a necessary portal into a deeper experience of prayer. In this deeper level of prayer, having emptied ourselves out, we are able to become inwardly still, inwardly silent, inwardly receptive. We open ourselves to receive and rest in God's grace, in the experience of God's love in whatever way it comes to us. One modern spiritual text tells us, "God's answer is always some form of peace."

This seems to be the experience Mother Teresa is pointing us to in prayer. In prayer, we open ourselves so completely to receiving God's love for us that we are filled to overflowing, and this overflow naturally pours through and from us into service to others. She once described herself as "a little pencil in the hand of a writing God, who is sending a love letter to the world." Through prayer we align our being and will with God's Being and Will. In this way, we become channels through which love—its tenderness, beauty, kindness, and peace—can be expressed into this world. In the simplest ways, we become a living demonstration that God and love exist and are real.

The world has perhaps never been in greater need of an infusion of love—an inclusive love and care that extends not only to those nearest to us but to the entire family of humankind and the family of Earth itself as a whole. So many of the serious problems that confront us— from political extremism, racialized hatred and fear, and the ongoing horror of war to biodiversity loss and the destruction caused by increasingly frequent extreme weather events; from widespread addiction to anxiety and depression, especially among the young—grow out of and reflect a deeply conditioned mindset of scarcity and fear.

Albert Einstein famously pointed out that problems can never be solved from the same level of consciousness that created them. Real transformation in the world can only happen through *transformed consciousness*. Vaclav Havel, the playwright, dissident, and first president of the Czech Republic, once wrote that without a global revolution in the sphere of human consciousness, nothing will change for the better, that all true change in the world must begin in the human heart.

Saints and sages throughout time and across religious and spiritual traditions have agreed that a consciousness, or mindset of fear, can only be transformed ("cast out") by a consciousness of love. And that transformation of consciousness, Mother Teresa tells us, starts with prayer.

Reb Zalman Schacter-Shalomi, father of the Jewish Renewal movement, once wrote that consciousness is like tofu, that it takes on the flavor of whatever it is marinated in. If we marinate our consciousness in love, it becomes *saturated* with love, and then love will naturally flow through us into the thoughts we think, the words we speak, the actions we take. That is, perhaps, the deepest purpose and function of prayer.

This is the invitation Mother Teresa extends to us through the simple, beautiful meditations in this book. May we take her message to heart, perhaps more deeply than ever before in our lives, that we too may become channels for God's healing and peace, pencils through which God can write a love letter to a world so clearly starving for love.

REV. DIANE BERKE, FOUNDER AND SPIRITUAL DIRECTOR
One Spirit Learning Alliance/One Spirit Interfaith Seminary
New York City, March 2023

INTRODUCTION

The woman we all knew as Mother Teresa was devoutly Catholic and profoundly devoted to Jesus. She expressed her ceaseless devotion in so many ways, central among them her well-known work with the poor and the sick. Less known expressions included her deep respect for all religions and her burning wish for all people to come closer to God. It was with a longing to reach as many souls as possible that she wrote, "I've always said we should help a Hindu become a better Hindu, a Muslim become a better Muslim, a Catholic become a better Catholic." And it was with a practical recognition of what works that she declared, "Everything starts from prayer."

It is in this spirit that the following collection of Mother Teresa's sayings if offered. I've selected and arranged them from many of Mother Teresa's prior writings to give the widest possible access to people with no clear path as well as to those with various inner paths. I have tried to glean pearls of inspiration that provide an ecumenical entry into a life of prayer. And I've framed a host of Mother Teresa's reflections within this topic of prayer.

While Mother Teresa did not fully undertake an

entirely universal approach herself, the basic direction she took was shown on the occasion she asked a wealthy person to build a mosque in Yemen, with the plea that the Muslim brothers and sisters there needed a place to meet God.

It is the same direction she took with one of her friends and biographers, Navin Chawla. She knew he was a non observant, nearly atheistic Hindu, yet not once over the years did she question his beliefs or his religion. But she did repeatedly, some might say incessantly, nudge him with the same question, "Have you begun to pray yet?"

Consider also one of the projects dearest to Mother Teresa's heart: her Homes for the Dying, where every person receives the last rites of his or her own tradition. She was overheard to whisper to one of the terminally ill, "You say a prayer in your religion, and I will say a prayer as I know it. Together we will say this prayer and it will be something beautiful for God." By the early 1980s, 17,000 people had died in these Homes. Seeing the peace and beauty of their deaths, she was sure that all these souls, whatever their faiths or sects, had gone straight to heaven.

For Mother Teresa, prayer was the universal way to God. Her own spiritual advisor and biographer Edward Le Joly drove this point home, observing that when a journalist approached her at an airport with the request, "Have you a message for the American people?" Mother Teresa didn't say "give more," or even "love one another more." Rather, she answered without hesitation, "Yes, they should pray more."

And so, let's be clear: The book you hold now gives the same answer by the same great spiritual leader and teacher, only in an extended form. Instead of her succinct response amidst the bustle of an airport, you have a set of meditations to be savored slowly in your home. It's a fuller, more developed version of the same basic counsel, the same basic plea: "Pray more."

Everything Starts from Prayer relates more directly to personal and private prayer than to ritual and community prayer. This is fitting, because everything depends on your own beginning. Praying as an individual is no substitute for for the spiritual nurturance, sharing, and guidance of communal practice and service. Yet we need to begin, again and again, on our own, digging within our own ground, making room for the grace that is always available to us. Our rote prayers and our prayers together can have great meaning as a pooling of devotional energies only when they're infused with the fire of individual souls—the sweet and profound energy our own sould release when they've caught fire.

When Dorothy Hunt was considering an idea that ultimately became the lovely Mother Teresa collection *Love: A Fruit Always in Season*, she asked permission to undertake the task. Mother Teresa's reply: "Make it a prayer." Make the very work a prayer. My one suggestion for reading this book is an echo of hers: Make it a prayer. The more seriously and openly you approach it, the more the words will penetrate. The more you bring your whole self to it with unhurried simplicity and receptivity, the more the thoughts and feelings behind the words will touch something deep inside you. And the more fully you connect with your own wish to be in the presence of the Eternal as you read, the more likely it will be that the holy meaning behind the words will spark something real in you.

In her wonderful book *A Simple Path*, Mother Teresa introduced readings from her Order's prayer book by suggesting that readers could replace "Jesus" with "God" in their prayers if they were not Christian. Similarly here, feel free to replace the word "God" with whatever works best for you in referring to a higher power in your life. The same should be urged for Mother Teresa's reference to God as "he" or "him," and of other traditional gender vocabulary herein. Please substitute words you find acceptable if these are off-putting in any way.

Mother Teresa spoke often of how utterly she relied on the power of prayer to connect her to God. Twenty-four hours a day, she'd say. And for emphasis, she sometimes added that if the day were longer, that's how much longer she'd need God's strength through prayer.

But then, what spiritual seeker has not depended on prayer? And what heart has not cried out, and not been better for having done so?

ANTHONY STERN, M.D.

THE NEED TO PRAY

Everything starts from prayer. Without asking God for love, we cannot possess love and still less are we able to give it to others. Just as people today are speaking so much about the poor but they do not know the poor, we too cannot talk so much about prayer and yet not know how to pray.

✦

You may be exhausted with work, you may even kill yourself, but unless our work is interwoven with love, it is useless. To work without love is slavery.

✦

People throughout the world may look different or have a different religion, education, or position, but they are all the same. They are the people to be loved. They are all hungry for love.

In most modern rooms you see an
electrical light that can be turned on by
a switch. But, if there is no connection
with the main power house, then there
can be no light. Faith and prayer is the
connection with God, and when that is
there, there is service.

✦

We have to possess before we can give.
He who has the mission of giving to
others must grow first in the knowledge
of God. He must be full of that
knowledge.

✦

To be able to give, you must have.

✦

Love, to be true, has to begin with God in
prayer. If we pray, we will be able to love,
and if we love, we will be able to serve.

Whatever religion we are, we must pray together. Children need to learn to pray and they need to have their parents pray with them.

✦

It is easy to love the people far away. It is not always easy to love those close to us. It is easier to give a cup of rice to relieve hunger than to relieve the loneliness and pain of someone unloved in our own home. Bring love into your own home, for this is where our love for each other must start.

✦

In one of the houses our sisters visited, a woman had been dead a long time before anyone knew it, and then they found out only because her corpse had begun to rot. Her neighbors didn't even know her name.

There is much suffering in the world—
very much. And this material suffering
is suffering from hunger, suffering from
homelessness, from all kinds of diseases,
but I still think the greatest suffering is
being lonely, feeling unloved, just having
no one.

✦

There are different kinds of poverty. In
India some people live and die in hunger.

But in the West you have another kind
of poverty, spiritual poverty. This is far
worse. People do not believe in God,
do not pray. People do not care for each
other. You have the poverty of people
who are dissatisfied with what they have,
who do not know how to suffer, who
give in to despair. This poverty of heart
is often more difficult to relieve and to
defeat.

I remember some time ago I visited a very wonderful home for old people. There were about forty there and they had everything, but they were all looking towards the door. There was not a smile on their faces, and I asked the sister in charge of them, "Sister, why are these people not smiling? Why are they looking towards the door?" And she, very beautifully, had to answer and give the truth: "It's the same every day. They are longing for someone to come and visit them." This is great poverty.

✦

When things become our masters, we are very poor.

✦

You and I have been created for greater things. We have not been created to just pass through this life without aim. And that greater aim is to love and be loved.

Some call him Ishwar, some call him
Allah, some simply God, but we all have
to acknowledge that it is He who made
us for greater things: to love and be loved.
What matters is that we love. We cannot
love without prayer, and so whatever
religion we are we must pray together.

✦

You will find Calcutta all over the world
if you have eyes to see.
The streets of Calcutta lead to every
man's door. I know that you may want to
make a trip to Calcutta, but it is easy to
love people far away. It is not always easy
to love people who live beside us. What
about the ones I dislike or look down
upon?

✦

It is easy to be proud and harsh and
selfish—so easy. But we have been
created for better things.

Once in a while we should ask ourselves
several questions in order to guide our
actions. We should ask questions like: Do
I know the poor? Do I know, in the first
place, the poor in my family, those who
are closest to me—people who are poor,
but not because they lack bread?

There are other types of poverty just as
painful because they are more intrinsic.

Perhaps what my husband or wife lacks,
what my children lack, what my parents
lack, is not clothes or food. Perhaps they
lack love, because I do not give
it to them!

✦

Where does love begin?
In our own homes.
When does it begin?
When we pray together.

We have to feed ourselves. We can die
of spiritual starvation. We must be filled
continually, like a machine. When one
little thing in the machine is not working,
then the whole machine is not working
properly.

✦

I am asked what is one to do to be sure
one is following the way of salvation. I
answer: "Love God. And, above all, pray."

2

STARTING WITH
SILENCE

It is very hard to pray if one does not
know how. We must help ourselves
to learn. The most important thing is
silence.

✦

We need to find God and God cannot be
found in noise and restlessness.

✦

We cannot place ourselves directly in
God's presence without imposing upon
ourselves interior and exterior silence.
That is why we must accustom ourselves
to stillness of the soul,
of the eyes,
of the tongue.

✦

There is no life of prayer without silence.

Everything begins with prayer that is
born in the silence of our hearts.

✦

If we really want to pray, we must first
learn to listen: for in the silence of the
heart God speaks.

✦

Silence of the *heart*, not only of the
mouth—that too is necessary. Then you
can hear God everywhere:
in the closing of the door,
in the person who needs you,
in the birds that sing,
in the flowers, the animals—
that silence which is wonder and praise.

The contemplatives and ascetics of all
ages and religions have sought God in the
silence and solitude of the desert, forest,
and mountain.

✦

We too are called to withdraw at
certain intervals into deeper silence
and aloneness with God, together as
a community as well as personally. To
be alone with him, not with our books,
thoughts, and memories but completely
stripped of everything, to dwell lovingly
in his presence—silent, empty, expectant,
and motionless.

Listen in silence, because if your heart is
full of other things you
cannot hear the voice of God. But when
you have listened to the voice of God
in the stillness of your heart, then your
heart is filled with God. This will need
much sacrifice, but if we really mean to
pray and want to pray we must be ready
to do it now.

✦

To foster and maintain a prayerful
atmosphere of exterior silence we shall

- respect certain times and places of more
  strict silence
- move about and work prayerfully, quietly
  and gently
- avoid at all costs all unnecessary speaking
  and notice
- speak, when we have to, softly, gently,
  saying just what is necessary
- look forward to profound silence as a
  holy and precious time, a withdrawal into
  the living silence of God.

We need silence to be alone with God, to
speak to him, to listen to him, to ponder
his words deep in our hearts. We need
to be alone with God in silence to be
renewed and to be transformed. Silence
gives us a new outlook on life. In it we
are filled with the grace of God himself,
which makes us do all things with joy.

✦

If we are careful of silence it will be easy
to pray.
There is so much talk,
so much repetition,
so much carrying on of tales in words and
in writing.
Our prayer life suffers so much because
our hearts are not silent.

Looking at your eyes I can tell whether
there is peace in your heart or not.

We see people radiating joy, and in their
eyes you can see purity. If we want our
minds to have silence, keep a silence of
the eyes. Use your two eyes to help you to
pray better.

✦

Man needs silence.

To be alone or together looking for God
in silence.

There it is that we accumulate the inward
power which we distribute in action, put
in the smallest duty and spend in the
severest hardships that befall us.

Silence came before creation, and the
heavens were spread without a word.

Interior silence is very difficult but we must make the effort. In silence we will find new energy and true unity. The energy of God will be ours to do all things well.

✦

These are only the first steps toward prayer, but if we never make the first step with determination, we will not reach the last one: the presence of God.

✦

If you sincerely want to learn to pray: keep silence.

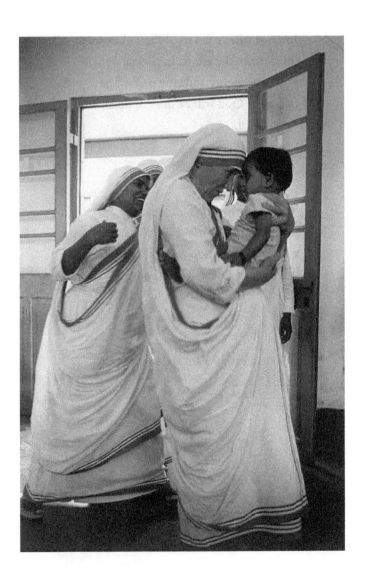

3

LIKE A LITTLE CHILD

My secret is a very simple one: I pray.

✦

Prayer is simply talking to God.
He speaks to us: we listen.
We speak to him: he listens.
A two-way process:
speaking and listening.

That is really prayer.
Both sides listening
and both sides speaking.

✦

Start and end the day with prayer. Come
to God as a child. If you find it hard to
pray you can say, "Come Holy Spirit,
guide me, protect me, clear out my mind
so that I can pray."

Wherever they are, the Missionaries of Charity start the day's work with the same prayer from their community prayer book:

Dear Lord, the Great Healer, I kneel before you, since every perfect gift must come from you. I pray, give skill to my hands, clear vision to my mind, kindness and meekness to my heart.
Give me singleness of purpose, strength to lift up a part of the burden of my suffering fellowmen, and a realization of the privilege that is mine. Take from my heart all guile and worldliness, that with the simple faith of a child, I may rely on you.
Amen.

How do you pray? You should go to God
like a little child. A child has no difficulty
expressing his mind in simple words that
say so much.

If a child is not yet spoiled and has
not yet learned to tell lies, he will tell
everything. This is what I mean by being
childlike.

✦

How do we learn to pray? By praying. It
is very hard to pray if one does not know
how. We must help ourselves to learn.
Pray with absolute trust in God's loving
care for you and let him fill you with joy
that you may preach without preaching.

✦

You can pray anytime, anywhere. You do
not have to be in a chapel or a church.

Love to pray—feel the need to pray often during the day and take the trouble to pray. If you want to pray better, you must pray more.

✦

The more you pray, the easier it becomes. The easier it becomes, the more you'll pray.

✦

You can pray while you work. Work doesn't stop prayer and prayer doesn't stop work. It requires only that small raising of the mind to him:
"I love you God, I trust you,
I believe in you, I need you now."
Small things like that.
They are wonderful prayers.

Often, under the pretext of humility, of
trust, of abandonment, we can forget to
use the strength of our will.
Everything depends on these words:
"I will" or "I will not."
And into the expression "I will"
I must put all my energy.

✦

We must know the meaning of the
prayers we say and feel the sweetness of
each word to make these prayers of great
profit; we must sometimes meditate on
them and often during the day find our
rest in them.

✦

You can say, "My Lord, I love You."
"My God, I am sorry."
"My God, I believe in You."
"My God, I trust You."
"Help us to love one another as You love
us."

You can pray for the works of others
and help them. For example, in our
community there are second self helpers
who offer their prayers for a sister
who needs the strength to carry on
her active work. And we also have the
contemplative sisters and brothers, who
pray for us all the time.

✦

"I kept the Lord ever before my eyes
because he is ever at my right hand that
I may not slip," says the psalmist. God is
within me with a more intimate presence
than that whereby I am in myself: in him
we live and move and have our being. It is
he who gives life to all, that gives power
and being to all that exists. But for his
sustaining presence, all things would
cease to be and fall back into nothingness.

Consider that you are in God,
surrounded and encompassed by God,
swimming in God.

✦

We need to help each other in our prayers.
Let us free our minds. Let's not pray long,
drawn-out prayers, but let's pray short
ones full of love. Let us pray on behalf of
those who do not pray. Let us remember, if
we want to be able to love, we must be able
to pray!

It is now seven hundred and fifty years
since St. Francis of Assisi composed the
following prayer for himself and for those
whom he taught to love God:

Lord, make me an instrument of your
peace.
Where there is hatred, let me sow love.
Where there is injury, let me sow pardon.
Where there is friction, let me sow union.
Where there is error, let me sow truth.
Where there is doubt, let me sow faith.
Where there is despair, let me sow hope.
Where there is darkness, let me sow light.
Where there is sadness, let me sow joy.

O Divine Master, grant that I may not so
much seek
To be consoled as to console,
To be understood as to understand, To
be loved as to love,
For it is in giving that we receive.
It is in pardoning that we are pardoned.
It is in dying that we are born to eternal
life.

We want so much to pray properly and
then we fail. We get discouraged and give
up on prayer. God allowed the failure
but he did not want the discouragement.
He wants us to be more childlike, more
humble, more grateful in prayer.

✦

Try speaking directly to God. Just speak.
Tell him everything,
talk to him. He is our father, he is father
to us all whatever religion we are. We
have to put our trust in him and love him,
believe in him, work for him. And if we
pray, we will get all the answers we need.

One of my favorite devotional songs is
called Only a Shadow. Its verses run like
this:

The love I have for you, my Lord
Is only a shadow of your love for me,
Your deep abiding love.
My own belief in you, my Lord,
Is only a shadow of your faith in me,
Your deep and trusting faith.
My life is in your hands.
My love for you will grow, my Lord.
Your light in me will shine.
The dream I have today, my Lord,
Is only a shadow of your dream for me,
If I but follow you.
The joy I feel today, my Lord,
Is only a shadow of your joys for me,
Only a shadow of all that will be
When we meet face to face.

There are some people who, in order not to pray, use as an excuse the fact that life is so hectic that it prevents them from praying.

This cannot be.

Prayer does not demand that we interrupt our work, but that we continue working as if it were a prayer.

It is not necessary to always be meditating, nor to consciously experience the sensation that we are talking to God, no matter how nice this would be. What matters is being with him, living in him, in his will.

God is purity himself; nothing impure
can come before him, but I don't think
God can hate, because God is love and
God loves us in spite of our misery.

God loves because he is love, but impurity
is an obstacle to seeing God.

✦

Our souls should be like a transparent
crystal through which God can be
perceived.

✦

Our crystal is sometimes covered with
dirt and dust. To remove this dust
we carry out an examination of our
conscience in order to obtain a clean
heart. God will help us to remove that
dust, as long as we allow him to: if that is
our will, his will comes about.

The more we empty ourselves, the more
room we give God to fill us.

✦

When we have nothing to give, let us give
him that nothingness.

✦

Riches, material or spiritual, can suffocate
you if they are not used in the right way.
Remain as "empty" as possible, so that
God can fill you.

✦

Even God cannot put anything into
what is already full. He does not impose
himself on us.

It is not how much we really have to give but how empty we are—so that we can receive fully in our life. Take away your eyes from yourself and rejoice that you have nothing—that you are nothing—that you can do nothing.

✦

We have to pray on behalf of those who do not pray.

✦

We should be professionals in prayer.

✦

Love to pray. Feel often during the day the need for prayer and take trouble to pray. God is always speaking to us. Listen to him.

Recreation is a means to pray better. Relaxation sweeps away the cobwebs of the mind.

✦

When you pray, give thanks to God for all his gifts because everything is his and a gift from him.

✦

Your soul is a gift of God.

✦

As long as we do not make the best effort we are capable of, we cannot feel discouraged by our failures. We cannot claim any successes either. We should give God all the credit and be extremely sincere when we do so.

Be sincere in your prayers.
Do you pray your prayers?
Do you know how to pray?
Do you love to pray?
Sincerity is nothing but humility and
you acquire humility only by accepting
humiliations.

✦

All that has been said about humility is
not enough to teach you humility. All
that you have read about humility is not
enough to teach you humility. You learn
humility only by accepting humiliations.
And you will meet humiliation all
through your lives.

The greatest humiliation is to know that
you are nothing. This you come to know
when you face God in prayer. When you
come face to face with God, you cannot
but know that you are nothing, that you
have nothing.

✦

If we really fully belong to God, then we
must be at his disposal and we must trust
in him. We must never be preoccupied
with the future. There is no reason to be
so. God is there.

✦

Yesterday is gone.
Tomorrow has not yet come.
We have only today.

Let us begin.

Don't search for God in far lands—he is
not there. He is close to you. He is with
you. Just keep the lamp burning and you
will always see him. Watch and pray.
Keep kindling the lamp and you will see
his love and you will see how sweet is the
Lord you love.

✦

Today, more than ever, we need to pray
for the light to know the will of God, for
the love to accept the will of God, for the
way to do the will of God.

✦

Pray lovingly like children, with an
earnest desire to love much and make
loved the love that is not loved.

Let us thank God for all his love for us, in
so many ways and in so many places.

May God give us all openness to ways
leading beyond our own selves.

✦

Prayer, to be fruitful, must come from the
heart and must be able to touch the heart
of God.

4

OPENING YOUR HEART

Open your hearts to the love of God
which he will give you. He loves you with
tenderness. And he will give you not to
keep but to share.

✦

Our prayers should be burning words
coming forth from the furnace of hearts
filled with love. In your prayers, speak to
God with great reverence and confidence.

✦

Do not drag behind or run ahead; do not
shout or keep silent, but devoutly, with
great sweetness, with natural simplicity,
without any affectation, offer your praise
to God with the whole of your heart and
soul.

We ought every day to renew our
resolution and to rouse ourselves to
fervor, as if it were the first day of our
conversion, saying, "Help me, Lord
God, in my good resolve and in thy holy
service, and give me grace this very day
really and truly to begin, for what I have
done till now is nothing."

✦

The prayer that comes from the mind and
heart and which we do not read in books
is called mental prayer. In vocal prayer we
speak to God; in mental prayer he speaks
to us. It is then that God pours himself
into us.

Mental prayer is greatly fostered by simplicity—that is, forgetfulness of self by transcending of the body and of our senses, and by frequent aspirations that feed our prayer. "In mental prayer," says Saint John Vianney, "shut your eyes, shut your mouth, and open your heart."

✦

Prayer enlarges the heart until it is capable of containing God's gift of himself. Ask and seek and your heart will grow big enough to receive him and keep him as your own.

✦

Offer to God every word you say, every movement you make. We must more and more fall in love with God.

We need prayers in order to better carry out the work of God, and so that in every moment we may know how to be completely available to him.

We should make every effort to walk in the presence of God, to see God in all the persons we meet, to live our prayer throughout the day.

✦

We must pray perseveringly and with great love.

✦

Love is a fruit in season at all times and within the reach of every hand. Anyone may gather it and no limit is set. Everyone can reach this love through meditation, the spirit of prayer and sacrifice, by an intense inner life.

Do we really live this life?

Loving should be as normal to us as living
and breathing, day after day until our
death.

✦

Am I a dark light? A false light? A
bulb without the connection, therefore
shedding no radiance?

Put your heart into being a bright light.

✦

It is not what we do or how much we do,
but how much love we put into the action
because that action is our love for God in
action.

✦

God speaks in the silence of our heart,
and we listen. And then we speak to God
from the fullness of our heart, and God
listens.

Even when we sin or make a mistake, let's allow that to help us grow closer to God. Let's tell him humbly, "I know I shouldn't have done this, but even this failure I offer to you."

✦

Our words are useless unless they come from the bottom of the heart.

✦

Give yourself fully to God. He will use you to accomplish great things on the condition that you believe much more in his love than in your weakness.

Is my heart so clean that I can see the face
of God in my brother, my sister who is
that black one, that white one, that naked
one, that one suffering from leprosy, that
dying one?

And this is what we must pray for.

✦

God dwells in us.
That's what gives him a beautiful power.
It doesn't matter where you are as long
as you are clean of heart. Clean of heart
means openness, that complete freedom,
that detachment that allows you to
love God without hindrance, without
obstacles.

Every night before you go to bed you
must make an examination of conscience
(because you don't know if you will
be alive in the morning!). Whatever is
troubling you, or whatever wrong you
may have done, you need to repair it. For
example, if you have stolen something,
then try to give it back.

✦

If you have hurt somebody, try to make
up to that person; do it directly. If you
cannot make up like that, at least then
make up with God by saying, "I'm very
sorry." This is important because just as
we have acts of love, we also must have
acts of contrition. You could say, "Lord,
I'm sorry for having offended you and I
promise you I will try not to offend you
again."

It feels good to be free of burdens, to
have a clean heart. Remember that God
is merciful, he is the merciful father to us
all. We are his children and he will forgive
and forget if we remember to do so.

✦

Examine your heart first, though, to see if
there is any lack of forgiveness of others
still inside, because how can we ask
God for forgiveness if we cannot forgive
others?

✦

People ask me what advice I have for
a married couple struggling in their
relationship. I always answer "Pray and
forgive;" and to young people who come
from violent homes, "Pray and forgive;"
and to the single mother with no family
support, "Pray and forgive."

Remember, if you truly repent, if you
really mean it with a clean
heart, you will be absolved in God's eyes.
He will forgive you if you truly confess.
So pray to be able to forgive those who
have hurt you or whom you don't like,
and forgive as you have been forgiven.

✦

Prayer is a joy.
Prayer is the sunshine of God's love,
prayer is hope of eternal happiness,
prayer is the burning flame of God's love
for you and for me. Let us pray for each
other, for this is the best way to love one
another.

✦

Today be the sunshine of God's love.

God is still love, he is still loving the
world. Today God loves the world so
much that he gives you and he gives
me to love the world, to be his love and
compassion.

✦

You may be exhausted with work, even
kill yourself, but unless your work is
interwoven with love, it is useless.

✦

We must all fill our hearts with great love.
Don't imagine that love, to be true and
burning, must be extraordinary.

✦

God loves each one of us with a most
tender and personal love. His longing for
me is dearer than my longing for him.

There is no limit to God's love. It is
without limit and its depth cannot be
sounded.

✦

The best way to show your gratitude to
God and people is to accept everything
with joy. A joyful heart is the normal
result of a heart burning with love.

✦

It is so easy to be proud, harsh, moody
and selfish, but we have been created for
greater things; why stoop down to things
that will spoil the beauty of our hearts?

In the silence of the heart God speaks.

What does God say to us? He says: "I
have called you by your name, you are
mine; water will not drown you, fire will
not burn you, I will give up nations for
you, you are precious to me, I love you.
Even if a mother could forget her child, I
will not forget you. I have carved you in
the palm of my hand."

✦

We cannot speak unless we have listened,
unless we have made our connection with
God. From the fullness of the heart, the
mouth will speak, the mind will think.

Just once, let the love of God take entire
and absolute possession of your heart;
let it become to your heart like a second
nature; let your heart suffer nothing
contrary to enter; let it apply itself
continually to increase this love of God
by seeking to please him in all things
and refusing him nothing; let it accept as
from his hand everything that happens
to it; let it have a firm determination
never to commit any fault deliberately
and knowingly or, if it should fail, to be
humbled and to rise up again at once—
and such a heart will pray continually.

5

ENDING IN SILENCE

Souls of prayer are souls of great silence.

✦

Silence is the beautiful fruit of prayer.
We must learn not only the silence of the
mouth but also the silence of the heart,
of the eyes, of the ears and of the mind,
which I call the five silences.

✦

God is the friend of silence. See how
nature—trees, flowers, grass—grows in
silence. See the stars, the moon and the
sun, how they move in silence.

✦

In that silence, he will listen to us; there
he will speak to our soul, and there we
will hear his voice.

The fruit of silence is faith.
The fruit of faith is prayer.
The fruit of prayer is love.
The fruit of love is service.
And the fruit of service is silence.

✦

In the silence of the heart God speaks. If
you face God in prayer and silence, God
will speak to you. Then you will know
that you are nothing. It is only when you
realize your nothingness, your emptiness,
that God can fill you with himself.

✦

Silence gives us a new way of looking at
everything. We need this silence in order
to touch souls.

God is the friend of silence.
His language is silence.
"Be still and know that I am God."

6

THE FRUIT OF PRAYER

The more we receive in silent prayer, the more we can give in our active life.

✦

The essential thing is not what we say, but what God says to us and through us.

All our words will be useless unless they come from within.

✦

You can do what I can't do.
I can do what you can't do.
Together we can do something beautiful for God.

We do not strive for spectacular actions. What counts is the gift of yourself, the degree of love you put into each of your deeds.

✦

We can do no great things— only small things with great love.

✦

The fruit of prayer is a deepening of faith.

✦

Be faithful in small things because it is in them that your strength lies.

✦

Prayer feeds the soul— as blood is to the body, prayer is to the soul—and it brings you closer to God.

When you become full of God, you
will do all your work well, all of it
wholeheartedly. And when you are full
of God, you will do everything well. This
you can do only if you pray, if you know
how to pray, if you love prayer, and if you
pray well.

✦

The more I go around, the better I
understand how very necessary it is for us
to pray the work, to make the work our
love for God in action.

✦

God may allow everything to go upside
down in the hands of a very talented
and capable person. Unless the work is
interwoven with love, it is useless.

Love is not something that fossilizes, but
something that lives. Works of love, and
declaring love, is the way to peace. And
where does this love begin?
Right in our own hearts.
We must know that we have been created
for greater things, not just to be a number
in the world, not just to go for diplomas
and degrees, this work and that work.

We have been created in order to love and
be loved.

✦

If we neglect prayer and if the branch is
not connected with the vine, it will die.
That connecting of the branch to the vine
is prayer. If that connection is there then
love is there, then joy is there, and we will
be the sunshine of God's love, the hope
of eternal happiness, the flame of burning
love.

This is the true reason for our existence:
to be the sunshine of God's love, to be the
hope of eternal happiness. That's all.

✦

The fruit of prayer is a clean heart and a
clean heart is free to love.

✦

When you have a clean heart it means
you are open and honest with God, you
are not hiding anything from him, and
this lets him take what he wants from
you.

The energy of God will be ours to do all things well, and so will the unity of our thoughts with his thoughts, the unity of our prayers with his prayers, the unity of our actions with his actions, of our life with his life.

Unity is the fruit of prayer, of humility, of love.

✦

The value of our actions corresponds exactly to the value of the prayer we make.

Never think that a small action done to your neighbor is not worth much. It is not how much we do that is pleasing to God, but how much love we put into the doing.

Make sure you know your neighbor, for that knowledge will lead you to great love and love to personal service.

✦

We impatiently await God's paradise, but we have in our hands the power to be in paradise right here and now.
Being happy with God means this:
to love as he loves,
to help as he helps,
to give as he gives,
to serve as he serves.

✦

Love accepts all and gives all. Love should be as natural as living and breathing.

In the silence of the heart, God speaks
and you have to listen. Then in the
fullness of your heart,
because it is full of God,
full of love,
full of compassion,
full of faith,
your mouth will speak.

✦

You may be writing, and the fullness of
your heart will come to your hand also.
Your heart may speak through writing.
Your heart may speak through your
eyes also. You know that when you look
at people they must be able to see God
in your eyes. If you get distracted and
worldly, then they will not be able to see
God like that. The fullness of our heart
is expressed in our eyes, in our touch, in
what we write, in what we say, in the way
we walk, the way we receive, the way we
need. That is the fullness of our heart
expressing itself in many different ways.

We do not roam, but we cultivate the
vagabond spirit of abandonment.
We have nothing to live on,
yet we live splendidly;
nothing to walk on,
yet we walk fearlessly;
nothing to lean on,
but yet we lean on God confidently;
for we are his own and he is our
provident father.

✦

We are called upon not to be successful,
but to be faithful.

We get so many visitors every day at
Mother House in Calcutta.
When I meet them I give each one my
"business card." On it is written:
*The fruit of prayer is faith; The fruit of faith
is love; The fruit of love is service; The fruit
of service is peace.*

This is very good "business!"

✦

At the Home for the Dying in Kalighat, a
visitor wondered
at the peace that pervaded everywhere.
I said simply: "God is here.
Castes and creeds mean nothing.
It does not matter that they are not of my
faith."

We ourselves feel that what we are doing is just a drop in the ocean. But if that drop was not there, I think the ocean would be less by that missing drop. We don't have to think in numbers.

We can only love one person at a time, serve one person at a time.

✦

Wherever God has put you, that is your vocation.
It is not what we do but how much love we put into it.

To the cast of a musical performance in
Calcutta, I said: "Your work and our work
complete each other. What we are doing
is needed in the world as never before.
You are giving them joy by your action
and we are doing the same by service.
And it is the same action whether you are
singing and dancing and we are rubbing
and scrubbing. You are filling the world
with the love God has given you."

✦

Joy shows from the eyes,
it appears when one speaks and walks.
It cannot be kept closed inside us.
It reacts outside.
When people find in your eyes
that habitual happiness,
they will understand that
they are the beloved children of God.

We are talking about the joy that comes
from union with God,
from living in his presence, because living
in his presence fills us with joy.

When I speak of joy, I do not identify it
with loud laughter or with noise.
This is not true happiness.
Sometimes it hides other things.

When I speak of happiness,
I refer to an inner and deep peace,
which shows itself in our eyes,
on our faces, in our attitudes,
in our gestures, in our promptness.

That is what I see happening: people
coming to meet each other
because of their need for God. The
wonderful thing about it is that there is
a religious atmosphere; they all speak
about God.

This is a great experience for me. I feel
that to bring all these people together
to talk about God is really wonderful. A
new hope for the world.

✦

There is a tremendous strength that
is growing in the world through this
continual sharing, praying together,
suffering together and working together.

We do nothing.
He does everything.
All glory must be returned to him.

God has not called me to be successful.
He called me to be faithful.

One day in Calcutta a man came with a prescription and said, "My only child is dying and this medicine can be brought only from outside of India." Just at that time, while we were still talking, a man came with a basket of medicine. Right on the top of that basket, there was this medicine.

If it had been inside, I would not have seen it. If he had come before, or if he had come afterward, I could not have seen it. But just at that time, out of the millions and millions of children in the world, God in his tenderness was concerned with this little child of the slums of Calcutta enough to send, just at that time, that amount of medicine to save that child.

I praise the tenderness and the love of God, because every little one, in a poor family or a rich family, is a child of God, created by the Creator of all things.

Let us thank God for all his love for us, in so many ways and in so many places.

Let us in return, as an act of gratitude and adoration, determine to love him.

✦

Holiness is not a luxury for the few; it is not just for some people.
It is meant for you and for me, for all of us.
It is a simple duty, because if we learn to love, we learn to be holy.

✦

We all have much to give, to share, to contribute wherever we find ourselves to be living.

Holiness starts in the home, by loving God and those around us for his sake.

Total surrender to God must come
in small details just as it comes in big
details. It's nothing but that single word,
"Yes, I accept whatever you give, and I
give whatever you take." And this is just a
simple way for us to be holy.

✦

We must not create difficulties in our
own minds. To be holy doesn't mean to
do extraordinary things, to understand
big things, but it is a simple acceptance,
because I have given myself to God,
because I belong to him—my total
surrender. He could put me here. He
could put me there. He can use me. He
cannot use me. It doesn't matter because
I belong so totally to him that he can do
just what he wants to do with me.

Make sure that you let God's grace work in your souls by accepting whatever he gives you, and giving him whatever he takes from you. True holiness consists in doing God's will with a smile.

✦

Our progress in holiness depends on God and on ourselves—on God's race and on our will to be holy. We must have a real living determination to reach holiness.

✦

We must not attempt to control God's actions. We must not count the stages in the journey he would have us make. We must not desire a clear perception of our advance along the road, nor know precisely where we are on the way of holiness.

Become holy. Each one of us has a
capacity to become holy and the way to
holiness is prayer.

✦

We treat all people as children of God.
They are our brothers and sisters. We
show great respect to them. Our work is
to encourage these people, Christians as
well as non-Christians, to do works of
love. Every work of love done with a full
heart brings people closer to God.

Every human being comes from the hand
of God, and we all know what is the love
of God for us.

God has his own ways and means to
work in the hearts of men and we do
not know how close they are to him but
by their actions we will always know
whether they are at his disposal or not.
Whether you are a Hindu, a Muslim or
a Christian, how you live your life is the
proof that you are fully his or not.

✦

Loving must be as normal to us as living
and breathing, day after day until our
death. To understand this and practice it
we need much prayer, the kind that unites
us with God and overflows continually
upon others.

Our works of charity are nothing but the
overflow of our love of God from within.
Therefore, the one who is most united to
him loves her neighbor most.

Let no one glory in their success but refer
all to God in deepest thankfulness; on the
other hand, no failure should dishearten
them as long as they have done their best.
God sees only our love.
God will not ask how many books we
have read,
how many miracles we have worked,
but whether we have done our best for
the love of him.
Have we played well?
Slept well?
Eaten well?
Nothing is small for God.

We are so small we look at things in a
small way. But God, being Almighty, sees
everything great. Therefore, even if you
write a letter for a blind man or you just
go and
sit and listen,
or you take the mail for him,
or you visit somebody
or bring a flower to somebody
—small things—or wash clothes for
somebody,
or clean the house.
Very humble work, that is where you and
I must be.
For there are many people who can do big
things.
But there are very few people who will do
the small things.

It is so beautiful that we complete each
other! What we are doing in the slums,
maybe you cannot do. What you are
doing in the level where you are called—
in your family life, in your college life,
in your work—we cannot do. But you
and we together are doing something
beautiful for God.

✦

Often you see small and big wires, new
and old, cheap and expensive electric
cables. Alone they are useless and until
the current passes through them there
will be no light.
The wire is you and me.
The current is God.

✦

We have the power to let the current pass
through us and use us to produce the
light of the world or we can refuse to be
used and allow the darkness to spread.

If you have learned how to pray, then I
am not afraid for you. If you know how
to pray, then you will love prayer—and
if you love to pray, then you will pray.
Knowledge will lead to love and love to
service.

✦

Among yourselves you can share your
own experience of your need to pray, and
how you found prayer, and what the fruit
of prayer has been in your own lives.

✦

Let us spread the good news that prayer
is our strength.

HOMILY OF HIS HOLINESS
POPE FRANCIS

HOLY MASS AND RITE OF CANONIZATION
OF BLESSED MOTHER TERESA OF CALCUTTA
SAINT PETER'S SQUARE, 4 SEPTEMBER 2016

"Who can learn the counsel of God?" (*Wis* 9:13). This question from the Book of Wisdom . . . suggests that our life is a mystery and that we do not possess the key to understanding it. There are always two protagonists in history: God and man. Our task is to perceive the call of God and then to do his will. But in order to do his will, we must ask ourselves, "What is God's will in my life?"

We find the answer in the same passage of the Book of Wisdom: "People were taught what pleases you" (*Wis* 9:18). In order to ascertain the call of God, we must ask ourselves and understand what pleases God. On many occasions the prophets proclaimed what was pleasing to God. Their message found a wonderful synthesis in the words "I want mercy, not sacrifice" (*Hos* 6:6; *Mt* 9:13). God is pleased by every act of mercy, because in the brother or sister that we assist, we recognize the face of God which no one can see (cf. *Jn* 1:18). Each time we bend down to the needs of our brothers and sisters, we give Jesus something to eat and drink; we clothe, we help, and we visit the Son of God (cf. *Mt* 25:40).

We are thus called to translate into concrete acts that which we invoke in prayer and profess in faith. There is no alternative to charity: those who put themselves at the service of others, even when they don't know it, are those who love God (cf. *1 Jn* 3:16-18; *Jas* 2:14-18). The Christian life, however, is not merely extending a hand in times of need. If it is just this, it can be, certainly, a lovely expression of human solidarity which offers immediate benefits, but it is sterile because it lacks roots. The task which the Lord gives us, on the contrary, is the *vocation to charity* in which each of Christ's disciples puts his or her entire life at his service, so to grow each day in love.

We heard in the Gospel, "Large crowds were travelling with Jesus" (*Lk* 14:25). Today, this "large crowd" is seen in the great number of volunteers who have come together for the Jubilee of Mercy. You are that crowd who follows the Master and who makes visible his concrete love for each person. I repeat to you the words of the Apostle Paul: "I have indeed received much joy and comfort from your love, because the hearts of the saints have been refreshed through you" (*Philem* 1:7). How many hearts have been comforted by volunteers! How many hands they have held; how many tears they have wiped away; how much love has been poured out in hidden, humble and selfless service! This praiseworthy service gives voice to the faith and expresses the mercy of the Father, who draws near to those in need.

Following Jesus is a serious task, and, at the same time,

one filled with joy; it takes a certain daring and courage to recognize the divine Master in the poorest of the poor and to give oneself in their service. In order to do so, volunteers, who out of love of Jesus serve the poor and the needy, do not expect any thanks or recompense; rather they renounce all this because they have discovered true love. Just as the Lord has come to meet me and has stooped down to my level in my hour of need, so too do I go to meet him, bending low before those who have lost faith or who live as though God did not exist, before young people without values or ideals, before families in crisis, before the ill and the imprisoned, before refugees and immigrants, before the weak and defenseless in body and spirit, before abandoned children, before the elderly who are on their own. Wherever someone is reaching out, asking for a helping hand in order to get up, this is where our presence—and the presence of the Church which sustains and offers hope—must be.

Mother Teresa, in all aspects of her life, was a generous dispenser of divine mercy, making herself available for everyone through her welcome and defense of human life, those unborn and those abandoned and discarded. She was committed to defending life, ceaselessly proclaiming that "the unborn are the weakest, the smallest, the most vulnerable." She bowed down before those who were spent, left to die on the side of the road, seeing in them their God-given dignity; she made her voice heard before the powers of this world, so that they might recognize their guilt for the crime of poverty they created. For Mother Teresa, mercy was the "salt" which gave flavour to her work, it was the "light" which shone in the darkness of the many who no longer had tears to shed for their poverty and suffering.

Her mission to the urban and existential peripheries remains for us today an eloquent witness to God's closeness to the poorest of the poor. Today, I pass on this emblematic figure of womanhood and of consecrated life to the whole world of volunteers: may she be your model of holiness! May this tireless worker of mercy help us to increasingly understand that our only criterion for action is gratuitous love, free from every ideology and all obligations, offered freely to everyone without distinction of language, culture, race or religion. Mother Teresa loved to say, "Perhaps I don't speak their language, but I can smile." Let us carry her smile in our hearts and give it to those whom we meet along our journey, especially those who suffer. In this way, we will open up opportunities of joy and hope for our many brothers and sisters who are discouraged and who stand in need of understanding and tenderness.

INTRODUCTION TO THE SECOND EDITION:

MOTHER TERESA'S FAITH AND DOUBT

ANTHONY STERN, M.D.

*S*ince the publication of this collection's first edition in 1998, letters written by Mother Teresa have revealed that she struggled with severe doubt due to a sense of inner distance from God. This has been a challenging and sobering revelation for people of faith who have idealized her. But ultimately, the revelation of Mother Teresa's inner struggle is a blessing—it undermines several pervasive myths about the spiritual journey, and it underscores a central and powerful truth about prayer.

First, Mother Teresa's doubt subverts the myth that holy people do not encounter crises and impasses. As children, we often put our elders and mentors on pedestals, but as we grow older, we come to see that the parents and leaders we admire all struggle and have a shadow side, no matter how holy, good, or beautiful they are. To discover the complexity of those we look up to is simply a part of growing up and becoming more aware adults.

Second, her struggle with inner doubt and darkness

reveals the myth that the spiritual journey is a bed of roses, all sweetness and light. "Tell me, Father," Mother Teresa wrote in a letter in 1959 to Reverend Lawrence Picachy, "why is there so much pain and darkness in my soul?"[1] Like any worthy undertaking, the path to the Source of all blessings, the Divine Mystery, involves serious difficulty at times and requires tremendous perseverance. This often manifests in excruciating loneliness and inner emptiness— an arid, desolate landscape. "I am told God loves me—" she once wrote in a letter addressed to Jesus, "and yet the reality of darkness & coldness & emptiness is so great that nothing touches my soul." For some such souls, this sense of "spiritual dryness," as she called it, can stretch on for a devastatingly long period of time. As Mother Teresa's letters suggest, this was indeed true for her. By some scholars' accounts, she carried on for a half-century in total devotion to Christ while traversing an inner landscape in which she felt total abandonment by him.[2]

Third, her inner state sheds light on the myth that our own feelings are the exclusive or even the primary judge of whether our inner work is going well. It is a common mistake to base the validity of any work, spiritual or otherwise, primarily on how we feel. For example, when we love someone, we do not necessarily feel this love at all times. This has led countless teachers to say, rightly, that love is not a feeling. It includes how we feel, but it is much more than that. More than anything, love is a commitment. Mother Teresa's example of fidelity to her beloved God in the face of her perceived abandonment by him is unsurpassed. Similarly, anyone who expects to feel better because of their dedication to the inner quest is going to have trouble sustaining an effort for the long haul. It is very good to listen to one's feelings, and we all need a good outlet to express them, but to put them center-stage misses the spiritual boat.

Fourth, Mother Teresa's disquiet reveals the myth that true faith is a stranger to doubt. Anyone who has studied the lives of the saints or other holy people can likely appreciate this fact. It is through its friction with the darkness of doubt that the light of faith slowly becomes stronger, deeper, brighter. Seasoned travelers—not only beginners—on the spiritual path struggle with doubt and darkness. One religious master expressed this well when he said that to break through to spiritual realization, one needs great faith, great doubt, and great determination to reconcile the two opposing forces.

Finally, Mother Teresa's doubts about God's existence leads us to a central truth about prayer: intentional prayer only makes sense because of the very fact that we harbor the tension of doubt within us. If our bones were not sending whispers of doubt to our hearts, there would be no need for prayer at all. In a state of utterly pure faith, there is effortless silence and courage and virtue and action, without any recourse whatsoever to deliberate prayer. Most seekers eventually have a taste or two of such blessed times, or perhaps more frequent experiences of it, but no one— not even the saints—can live there all the time. The main point of prayer is that it strengthens our faith in the face of doubt, wherever we are on the sinner-saint spectrum.

In other words, doubt is inevitable. If we did not doubt, we would not be human. All human beings face pain and are prone to uncertainty, to that "terrible darkness,"[3] as Mother Teresa once described it. The question is: what do we do with this knot of pain and confusion within us? Do we get entirely lost in it, or do we accept it and oppose it and gently work to transform it through our spiritual intention and practice? We face this choice every day, just as she did. This is our spiritual training. And just as with any learning process, some days and some hours we do better than others. If we can accept this reality, we can perhaps learn more and more profoundly to be patient with ourselves. For many of us—from the spiritual leader to the nascent seeker—reaching higher ground involves that familiar dance of two steps forward, one step back. We continue progressing toward something closer to perfection while accepting our imperfections. A fitting illustration of this journey, prayer itself embodies a healthy combination of sincere aspiration tempered by honest acceptance.

In this sense, all of our prayers, even those of gratitude and thanksgiving, can be seen as echoes of the father of the epileptic son in the Gospel of Mark, who cried out from his heart to Jesus, "I believe, please help my unbelief!" In other words, "I have faith, please help my doubt!" This is an honest human prayer. Perhaps it is *the* honest human prayer, expressed in many ways. Prayer is an embodiment of the faith and the doubt alive within all of us.

Mother Teresa's doubt makes her more alive today than ever. Her honest human prayer serves as a beacon for people of all faiths, in all walks of life, who traverse that lonely and arid landscape. "If I ever become a Saint," she wrote in 1962, "I will surely be one of 'darkness.' I will continually be absent from Heaven—to [light] the light of those in darkness on earth."[4] As we imagine her lighting the light in her faithful vigil over us, let us also pray for her and all the saints, for all of our teachers and mentors, and "let us pray for each other, for this is the best way to love one another."[5] The title of this work is taken from Mother Teresa's own words: "Everything starts from prayer." Although prayer was, at times, difficult for her, I believe it was a cornerstone of her astounding faith in the face of persistent doubt. In our own prayers, may we all proceed together in a deepening bond of mutual love and support, helping each other with the pain and the doubt that is our common lot, and may we continue to grow in compassion for each other.

Endnotes

[1] David Van Biema, "Mother Teresa's Crisis of Faith," *Time*, August 23, 2007, http://www.time.com/time/world/article/0,8599,1655415-2,00.html

[2] Ibid.

[3] "Letters reveal Mother Teresa's doubt about faith," Reuters India, August 25, 2007, http://in.reuters.com/article/topNews/idINIndia-29140020070824?pageNumber=3&virtualBrandChannel=0

[4] David Van Biema, "Mother Teresa's Crisis of Faith," *Time*, August 23, 2007, http://www.time.com/time/world/article/0,8599,1655415-2,00.html

[5] *Everything Starts from Prayer*, page 88.

FOREWORD TO THE FIRST EDITION

*P*rayer is one of the most essential activities of human life. Throughout history it has nurtured our grandest visions and provided meaning and purpose to our activities. It is impossible to imagine the evolution of any culture without prayer. Prayer is universal; we know of no society where it does not take place.

Prayer has many faces. There are prayers of petition, intercession, thanksgiving, and adoration. But one thread connects all prayer: Whatever form it may take, *prayer is a bridge to the Absolute,* a way of connecting with something higher, wiser, and more powerful than the individual self.

Many people believe that prayer is too old-fashioned in our modern, scientific age, that prayer and science are incompatible, and that prayer belongs to the category of superstition and fantasy. One of the great ironies of the modern age, however, is that proponents of prayer and proponents of science are engaged in a new and amazing dialogue. This is happening in three different ways.

First, a high proportion of current scientists today believe in a Supreme Being who answers prayer. This may come as a shock to people who have been taught that genuine scientists cannot simultaneously believe in the Absolute and do good science. In 1997, however, researchers surveyed American biologists, physicists, and mathematicians about their religious beliefs.[1] They found that 39% believe in God—specifically, they believe in the kind of God who responds to prayer. The highest percentage of believers was found among mathematicians, who practice what many consider the purest kind of science that exists. And so we see that the prevalent views that science is godless, that atheists make the best scientists, and that prayer and science cannot coexist are simply stereotypes to be challenged.

Second, medical scientists studying the effects of prayer have found compelling evidence of the benefits of prayer, meditation, and relaxation on individuals who pray.[2] The body appears to *like* prayer and responds in healthy ways in the cardiovascular, immune, and other systems. But even more interesting are studies showing that intercessory or *distant* prayer also has an effect, even when the individual being prayed for is unaware of the prayer being offered and is at a great distance from the person praying. These studies are numerous, have been replicated by many scientists, and have involved not only humans but nonhumans as the prayer recipients. This latter point is important: If prayer's effects extend to animals and plants, they cannot be ascribed only to positive thinking or the placebo response.

The third major development heralding a synthesis of science and prayer is the recent emergence of scientific theories on the nature of consciousness.[3] In general, these views go beyond the old idea that the effects of the mind are confined to one's individual brain and body. These new theories permit consciousness to act outside the physical body, perhaps through intercessory prayer. In light of these new ways of thinking about consciousness, it no longer seems outrageous to suggest that prayer might act at a distance to bring about actual changes in the world.

In studies of intercessory prayer, researchers have found no correlation between the religious affiliation of the praying individual and the effects of prayer. This affirms the view that prayer is universal, that it belongs not just to a specific religion but to the entire human race. These findings sanction the importance of religious tolerance, asking us to honor the prayers and spiritual visions of other religious traditions, no matter how radically they may differ from our own.

Although personal religion does not correlate with prayer's effects in experimental studies, there is a quality that does make a great difference. It is a factor that sounds quite old-fashioned: *love*. Without love, the prayer experiments don't work as well; in fact, they often fall flat. As a physician, this finding intrigues me, because healers throughout history have uniformly proclaimed the importance of compassion, caring, and empathy for the patient. The best physicians I know honor the power of love and care in healing. They believe that, while penicillin may be powerful, penicillin plus love is more powerful still.

It is on these two issues in particular—the role of religious tolerance and the place of love and compassion in prayer—that I feel especially connected with Mother Teresa's work and writings. As Tony Stern points out in his introduction to this volume, Mother Teresa stated, "I've always said we should help a Hindu become a better Hindu, a Muslim become a better Muslim, a Catholic become a better Catholic."

There is a related story about Mother Teresa that attests to her tolerance, one that I have always adored, although it may be apocryphal. A brash young reporter once asked her, "Are you a saint?" Without hesitating, she poked the young man in the chest with a gnarled finger and said, "Yes, and so are you!" Mother Teresa would undoubtedly insist that prayer does not need science to validate it, and I would agree. People test prayer every day in their lives, and life is the most important experimental laboratory of all. But, since science is one of the most powerful factors guiding modern life, we would be foolish to disregard what science has to say about prayer, particularly since so much of its current comments are positive.

One of the most remarkable trends in modern medicine is the return of prayer.[4] Three years ago, only three medical schools in the United States had courses exploring the role of religion and spiritual practice in health; currently, nearly thirty do.[5] First-rate researchers are examining the effects of prayer in healing at various medical schools, hospitals, and research institutions; national conferences linking spirituality and healthcare are becoming routine.

Somewhere, Mother Teresa must be smiling.

LARRY DOSSEY, M.D.
Executive Editor of Alternative Therapies *and author of* Healing Words, Prayer Is Good Medicine, *and* Be Careful What You Pray For

Endnotes

[1] E.J. Larson, "Scientists are still keeping the faith," *Nature* (April 3, 1997): 345.

[2] Larry Dossey, Healing Words: *The Power of Prayer and the Practice of Medicine* (San Francisco: HarperSanFrancisco, 1993).

[3] Larry Dossey, "Emerging Theories" in *Be Careful What You Pray For* (San Francisco: HarperSanFrancisco, 1997): 190-92.

[4] Larry Dossey, "The return of prayer," *Alternative Therapies* 3:6 (1997): 10ff.

[5] Jeffrey S. Levin, David B. Larson, Christina M. Puchalski, "Religion and spirituality in medicine: research and education," *Journal of the American Medical Association* 278 (1997): 792-93.

RETREAT RESOURCES

Mother Teresa advocates taking periods of time away from one's routine, even one's regular spiritual routine, to develop and renew a life of prayer. Perhaps the best place to begin looking for retreats is by asking local friends, family members, spiritual advisors, or trusted community leaders what ones they may be able to suggest.

Sometimes people need to travel far and wide to find where they're going. Here are a few places you can contact as further resources; needless to say, using Google or another search engine can lead you to a lot more information about these centers.

1) Contemplative Outreach National Office (Butler, NJ)—an outgrowth of the "Centering Prayer" movement, and particularly Father Thomas Keating's work. Primarily Catholic in its roots, but open to others. Phone: 973-838-3384.

2) Pendle Hill (Wallingford, PA)—a Quaker retreat center with a strong inter-faith history. Phone: 800-742-3150.

3) Shalem Institute (Bethesda, MD)—an ecumenical Christian center founded by an Episcopal priest, Tilden Edwards. Phone: 301-897-7334.

4) Retreats International (Notre Dame, IN)—a Catholic clearinghouse of retreat information that offers programs and publications, including a directory listing hundreds of retreat centers. Phone: 574-631-7800.

For a useful listing of many other centers for prayer and meditation, you may wish to consult *Sanctuaries: A Guide to Lodgings in Monasteries, Abbeys, and Retreats*, written by Jack and Marcia Kelly. Most of the places described are "contemplative communities which invite people to share their life and prayer," and generally they welcome people of all faiths, though they themselves grow out of particular traditions. Christian, Buddhist, Hindu, Sufi, and Jewish communities are represented. There are three books in this superb series, all published by Bell Tower in New York: *The Complete United States, The Northeast,* and *The West Coast and Southwest.*

FURTHER READING

The following list includes mostly books currently in print at the time of this writing—for the purpose of providing suggestions that will be most easily accessible to the reader, and also to keep the list within bounds. For this second edition, I have included two more recent works in the section describing Christian books on prayer; but otherwise, these are all works whose publication precedes the first edition printing in 1998.

BOOKS OF MOTHER TERESA'S SPIRITUAL WISDOM

These works can be divided into two categories: relatively small "gems" (volumes aimed at offering a good but limited sampling of thoughts) and books striving to be more definitive. All are explicitly Christ-centered (some more centrally than others), and all treat Mother Teresa's thoughts on prayer as one of at least a few themes. Primarily biographical works are beyond the scope of this bibliography.

Slimmer Books

In the Heart of the World: Thoughts, Prayers, and Stories (New World Library, Novato, CA, 1997). A fine edition of luminous selections edited by Becky Benenate.

Meditations from A Simple Path (Ballantine Books, NY, 1996). Excerpts from the larger book, *A Simple Path* (see below), composed entirely of Mother Teresa's own words and spiritual teaching. Another lovingly produced gift edition brimming with Mother Teresa's timeless pearls of wisdom.

In My Own Words (Gramercy Books, NY, 1996). Pearls arranged according to fifteen themes. Edited by Jose Luis Gonzalez-Balado, one of the long-standing editors of Mother Teresa's written works.

Words to Love By, compiled by Frank J. Cunningham (Ave Maria Press, Notre Dame, IN, 1983). Poetically presented text highlighting the glories and challenges of Mother Teresa's message, with frequent photos.

The Best Gift is Love: Meditations by Mother Teresa (Servant Publications, Ann Arbor, MI, 1982). Like *Words to Love By* in its basic approach—highlights of Mother Teresa's instructions and reflections, poetically presented on the page, with many photos interspersed. Compiled by Sean-Patrick Lovett.

Blessings of Love (Servant Publications, Ann Arbor, MI, 1996). A sweet collection of brief inspirational sayings gathered from several of the other Servant Publication works listed below. Edited by Nancy Sabbag.

A Gift for God: Prayers and Meditations (Harper San Francisco, San Francisco, CA, U.S. edition, 1975). One of the earliest short collections of reflections, and a kind of companion work to Malcolm Muggeridge's classic 1971 biographical sketch *Something Beautiful for God.*

Larger Works

No Greater Love (New World Library, Novato, CA, 1997). A wonderfully comprehensive and accessible collection organized in eleven themes, followed by a conversation with Mother Teresa and a biographical sketch. Edited by Becky Benenate and Joseph Durepos; foreword by Thomas Moore. Also now available in the U.S. in a Spanish edition (*El Amor Mas Grande*).

A Simple Path (Ballantine Books, NY, 1995). A perfect introduction to Mother Teresa's work and teachings, this book contains not only Mother Teresa's spiritual principles but also the experiences of them by other members of her Order and volunteers. Compiled and introduced by Lucinda Vardey. Contains an appendix with important dates in Mother Teresa's life and another with information on the Order she founded, the Missionaries of Charity.

My Life for the Poor (Harper and Row, New York, NY, 1985), edited by Jose Luis Gonzalez-Balado and Janet N. Playfoot. A series of autobiographical stories, outlining the arc of Mother Teresa's life, with many jewels of her central teachings embedded within it.

The Joy in Loving: A Guide to Daily Living with Mother Teresa (Viking Penguin, NY, original copyright in India 1996). Reflections, one for each day of the year, covering a wide range of topics. Two long-time associates of Mother Teresa's, Jaya Chaliha and Father Edward Le Joly, compiled this stirring collection. Father Le Joly, who was Mother Teresa's spiritual advisor and the author of a major biography of Mother Teresa, also provides a detailed introduction to the history of her work. The thoughts are presented as short sayings in stanza form. While not organized by theme, contains a useful thematic index. These editors published *Reaching Out in Love: Stories Told by Mother Teresa* in 2000 (Continuum), also strongly recommended.

Love: A Fruit Always in Season (Ignatius Press, San Francisco, CA, 1987). A far-ranging book of daily meditations, arranged according to the Catholic calendar and also by theme. An excellent selection edited by Dorothy S. Hunt, drawing upon many earlier works, all of which are cited—a real help for knowing where the meditations first appeared.

Total Surrender (Servant Publications, Ann Arbor, MI, 1985). A rich spiritual sourcebook of excerpts from the constitution of Mother Teresa's Order as well as her instructions and letters within the Order. Comprehensive. Edited by Brother Angelo Devananda.

Jesus: The Word to be Spoken: Meditations for Every Day of the Year (Servant Publications, Ann Arbor, MI, 1986). Another well-done collection by Brother Angelo Devananda, this one arranged in calendar form.

One Heart Full of Love (Servant Publications, Ann Arbor, MI, original copyright in Spain 1984). A variety of rousing talks, interviews, and correspondence, with an emphasis on loving the poor and the blessings of sharing. Edited by Jose Luis Gonzalez-Balado.

Loving Jesus (Servant Publications, Ann Arbor, MI, 1991). Another collection of dynamic addresses edited by Jose Luis Gonzalez-Balado, including a long interview and a biographical sketch.

Heart of Joy: The Transforming Power of Self-Giving (Servant Publications, Ann Arbor, MI, 1987). Yet another worthwhile Gonzalez-Balado compendium of Mother Teresa's words, gathered from a variety of sources.

Prayertimes with Mother Teresa: A New Adventure in Prayer Involving Scripture, Mother Teresa, and You (Image Books, New York, NY, 1989). For each week of the year, a passage from the Bible, a story by or about Mother Teresa, and a spiritual reflection from her. Edited by Eileen and Kathleen Egan. The main text is followed by a "seven-day retreat" section with suggested prayers, litanies, and meditations.

Works of Love Are Works of Peace: Mother Teresa of Calcutta and the Missionaries of Charity (Ignatius Press, San Francisco, 1996). One of the stunning books of photos available, this one has selections of Mother Teresa's counsel, including a letter on prayer, as well as a full collection of the Order's prayers.

Among other closely related books of interest, perhaps most notable is *Suffering into Joy* by Eileen and Kathleen Egan, (Servant Publications), which contains passages from Mother Teresa's teachings. See above for publisher's information.

FURTHER BOOKS ON PRAYER

There are many good books on prayer. The list below is far from exhaustive but includes some of this editor's favorite ones. They are restricted to books entirely about prayer, rather than ones that may contain a chapter or two on the subject. The emphasis is on practical, down-to-earth guides that are most likely to further the actual practice of prayer. Books of prayers are not included.

Books Addressed Equally to Christians and Non-Christians

Larry Dossey, *Prayer Is Good Medicine* (Harper San Francisco, San Francisco, CA, 1996). The author, who wrote the Foreword to *Everything Starts from Prayer* and is a highly regarded physician and thinker, describes this book as "a heart-to-heart talk."

Dossey wisely discusses prayer and common misconceptions about prayer, with a special focus on the relations between prayer, healing, and science. The longest of four sections is called "How to Pray." (See also Dossey's more detailed, scholarly *Healing Words: The Power of Prayer and the Practice of Medicine* and his more recent thoughtful book *Be Careful What You Pray For*.)

James P. Carse, *The Silence of God: Meditations on Prayer* (Harper San Francisco, San Francisco, CA, 1985). An NYU professor of religion brings simplicity together with philosophic depth to his writings on prayer. Four graceful, grounded meditations about speaking to God. Incisive yet subtly heart-centered.

Richard Chilson, *You Shall Not Want: A Spiritual Journey Based on the Psalms* (Ave Maria Press, Notre Dame, IN, 1996). A guide to prayer using brief selections and phrases from the psalms arranged for the thirty days in a month. Gently presented. From Ave Maria's "30 Days with a great Spiritual Teacher" Series, whose other volumes are also recommended.

Matthew Fox, *On Becoming a Musical Mystical Bear: Spirituality American Style* (Paulist Press, New York, NY, 1972). Simultaneously whimsical and serious, Fox takes a contemplative activist's look at "what prayer is" and "what prayer isn't." He presents his ideas of "creation spirituality" in the process, and whereas he doesn't present prayer here in the precise "how to" terms of a spiritual practice, he underscores points that many people inclined to withdraw from the world in the name of "dedicated spiritual practice" all too easily overlook.

Dale Salwak (editor) *The Power of Prayer* (New World Library, Novato, CA, 1999). A multifaith anthology that includes contributions by Mother Teresa and this editor. (Currently out of print but worthwhile finding used on the Internet.) Also see *The Flowering of the Soul: A Book of Prayers by Women* (Lucinda Vardey, editor), which offers an approach to praying through experiences and counsel of women from diverse traditions, including Mother Teresa.

Christian Books on Prayer

If you don't feel entirely comfortable calling yourself "Christian," yet you begin to read Christian writings, here's a suggestion: consider a different name that works for you. If the term "Christian" doesn't feel like a full fit, when you come across it on the page, substitute "a truly good person," "an open and growing person," "a holy person," "a person trying her or his very best," "a student of prayer," or "a sincere spiritual seeker." Where devotion to Jesus is discussed, this may not quite hit the mark, but where universal insights about devotion, prayer, and inner work are the subjects, it will. There may be legitimate objections to this idea. Nonetheless, it seems that "Christian" or other designations like "Jew" or "Muslim" are often used within their own groups as synonyms for "a truly good person." When used as such, they are a residue of a more provincial era. Let's try at times to open ourselves to writings of our brothers and sisters in other cultures, and to translate basic insights across these differing traditions, for the sake of discovering our common humanity, our common soul.

Henri J.M. Nouwen, *The One Necessary Thing: Living a Prayerful Life* (Crossroad, NY, original copyright 1999). This book is similar to the present collection, in that it is a labor of love compiled by my late friend Wendy Wilson Greer, bringing together Nouwen's thoughts on prayer from his diverse range of books. Greer was a good friend of Nouwen's, and Nouwen, a Catholic priest who died in 1996, is rightly cherished as one of the finest modern writers about the spiritual journey.

Metropolitan Anthony (Anthony Bloom), Volume in *The Modern Spirituality Series* (Templegate, Springfield, IL, 1987). The most concise introduction to a first-rate contemporary writer on prayer. The author was a former medical doctor and French resistance fighter turned Russian Orthodox priest and church leader who died in 2003. ("Metropolitan" is something like "Cardinal" in the Eastern Orthodox church.) The book is an offering of page-long selections from earlier works, and it contains a convenient reference to all of these works at the end, among which *Beginning to Pray* and *Living Prayer* are especially recommended.

Douglas V. Steere, *Dimensions of Prayer* (Upper Room Books, Nashville, TN, original copyright 1962). A succinct and down-to-earth classic on prayer by a scholar and Quaker leader. Steere, a philosophy professor at Haverford, was the main Quaker representative at Vatican II and an early pioneer of ecumenical dialogue with Buddhists and

Hindus. A document he wrote for Quaker organizational purposes eventually became the blueprint for the Peace Corps. He shares with Metropolitan Anthony a great gift for the telling vignette.

Thomas Keating, *Open Mind, Open Heart: The Contemplative Dimension of the Gospel* (Element Books, Rockport, ME, 1994). In 1975, a few Catholic monks came together and crafted a method called "centering prayer." Father Keating provides one of the clearest step-by-step descriptions of this approach, which simplifies age-old spiritual wisdom meaningfully for our time. Among its best points, Keating offers sound advice regarding "distracting thoughts" and inner obstacles to praying in general. It should be emphasized that the approach outlined is a high form of practice that isn't meant to exclude other forms. See also M. Basil Pennington's *Centering Prayer* and William A. Meninger's *The Loving Search for God*.

Philip Yancey, *Prayer: Does It Make Any Difference?* (Zondervan, Grand Rapids, MI, 2006). This is the most recent book in the bibliography. Yancey never disappoints. Like Richard Foster, whose own superb book on prayer is listed below, Yancey is highly intelligent and articulate, and he has thought seriously as a Christian about matters of the spirit for a long time. His honest vulnerability is perhaps his greatest gift to us. The "Prayer Resources" at the book's end offers Yancey's own annotated listing of Christian books about prayer and is more up-to-date than my own.

Ken Gire (editor), *Between Heaven and Earth: Prayers and Reflections That Celebrate An Intimate God* (Harper San Francisco, San Francisco, CA, 1997). An unusually good collection of reflections about prayer interspersed with some prayers themselves. Passages are mainly from well-known writers like C.S. Lewis, Richard Foster, Abraham Joshua Heschel, Larry Dossey, Dietrich Bonhoeffer, and many others you may well recognize. Various faith traditions are included, though the sources are primarily Christian.

Among the numerous other noteworthy Christian books about prayer as spiritual practice, please keep in mind the following titles: Brother David Steindl-Rast, *Gratefulness, The Hearth of Prayer: An Approach to Life in Fullness*; Richard J. Foster, *Prayer: Finding the Heart's True Home*; Tilden Edwards, *Living in Presence: Spiritual Exercises to Open Your Life to the Awareness of God*; Martin Helldorfer, *Prayer When It's Hard to Pray*; Thomas Kelly, *A Testament of Devotion*; Richard J. Foster and James Bryan Smith, *Devotional Classics*; Thomas Merton, *Contemplative Prayer* (the introduction by Zen master Thich Naht Hanh and foreword by Douglas Steere are treats in themselves); Gabriel Galache, *Praying Body and Soul: Methods and Practices of Anthony De Mello*; John R. Yungblut, *Rediscovering Prayer*; and Patricia Loring, *Listening Spirituality* (available from the Pendle Hill online store).

Jewish Books on Prayer

The note about the word "Christian" above applies equally to the word "Jew." Even as we honor our own traditions, we need to remember that historically a wounded antagonism has separated groups of believers and has colored their views of other groups. We need not only to remember, but also to forget: to do our utmost to acknowledge it in ourselves, work with it, and slowly (or immediately!) get beyond it. Let's not, in any case, deprive ourselves of the inspiration and insight contained in other sacred traditions, even in works purportedly aimed only at a single group of believers.

Arthur Green and Barry W. Holtz (editors and translators), *Your Word Is Fire: The Hasidic Masters on Contemplative Prayer* (Jewish Lights Publishing, Woodstock, VT, 1977). Parables and sayings from the extraordinary Hasidic literature on prayer, presented in verse form, with a brief introduction that serves admirably as a summary of Hasidic thought. Edited by two leaders of the Jewish renewal movement.

Yitzhak Buxbaum, *Real Davvening: Jewish Prayer as a Form of Meditation for Beginning and Experienced Davveners* (Jewish Spirit, New York, 1996). "Davvening" is a Jewish word for praying. This booklet explicitly aims to provide the reader hints for meeting God in prayer. In other words, it offers an explanation of the spiritual side of Jewish worship and contains simple traditional techniques for how to experience God's presence during communal devotional services. Readily applicable to other traditions. See also Buxbaum's much more detailed work, *Jewish Spiritual Practices*, especially chapters five and six. Google "Jewish Spirit" to buy these works online. Buxbaum is a dedicated teacher as well as a good friend of the editor's.

Rabbi Nachman, *Tsohar* ("Light") (Breslov Research Institute, New York, NY, 1986). The 18th and 19th century Hasidic tradition is a wonderful source of practical wisdom about prayer, and Rabbi Nachman of Breslov (or "Bratslav") was one of its greatest teachers. This booklet, which centers on the power of "just one true word" in prayer, is one of several valuable booklets published by The Breslov Research Institute. Other recommended ones include *Outpouring of the Soul* and *Restore My Soul*.

Sidney Greenburg, *A Treasury of Thoughts on Jewish Prayer* (Jason Aronson, Northvale, NJ, 1989). A rich anthology of short selections from many sources, including the Talmud, the Hasidic masters, and contemporary thinkers. These are intelligently selected and heartfelt passages with a scope wider than the question "how to pray"—but consistently good food for thought and inspiration for worship.

Islamic Books on Prayer

Prayer is central to Islamic spirituality. One of the five "pillars" of Islam is daily prayer (*salat*), which consists of a series of movements enacted while reciting suras, or chapters, from the Qur'an. Other forms of prayer include *du'a*, or personal entreaties and petitions; *dhikr*, or meditative remembrance on a sacred word or phrase; and *munajat*, or devotional conversations between lover and the divine beloved. A helpful introduction and sourcebook to prayer in Islam: Constance Padwick, *Muslim Devotions: A Study of Prayer Manuals in Common Use* (Oneworld Publications, Oxford, England, 1996; original copyright 1961).

SOURCES & ACKNOWLEDGMENTS

Wholehearted appreciation is due Sister Priscilla and the Missionaries of Charity in Calcutta for granting permission for the compilation of this collection and for their input in the process. A portion of the receipts from the sale of this book will go to the Missionaries of Charity. For more information on the work of the Order, search online or contact one of its U.S. houses: 335 E. 145th St., Bronx, NY 10451 and 1596 Fulton St., San Francisco, CA 94117.

I have tried to leave no stone unturned in my efforts to obtain permissions. If there are oversights I would request that the aggrieved party contact me so that I may get it right for the third edition.

It should be mentioned that there is a considerable overlap in Mother Teresa's writings. I have cited one source for each passage in this volume, but many of these meditations can be found in a few different books.

Where sources have been printed in hardcover and paperback editions, the page numbers below refer to the hardcover edition.

Grateful acknowledgements to:

New World Library for permission to reprint from the following seven works: *No Greater Love* (called simply "Love" below) (New World Library, New York, NY, 1997), edited by Becky Benenate and Joseph Durepos; *Total Surrender* (called simply "Surrender" below) (Servant Books, Ann Arbor, MI, 1985), edited by Brother Angelo Devananda; *Jesus, the Word to Be Spoken: Prayers and Meditations for Every Day of the Year* (called simply "Jesus" below) (Servant Books, Ann Arbor, MI, 1986), compiled by Brother Angelo Devananda; *Heart of Joy* (called simply "Heart" below) (Servant Books, Ann Arbor, MI, 1987), edited by Jose Luis Gonzalez-Balado; *One Heart Full of Love* (called simply "Full" below) (Servant Books, Ann Arbor, MI, 1984), edited by Jose Luis Gonzalez-Balado; *Loving Jesus* (called simply "Loving" below) (Servant Books, Ann Arbor, MI, 1991), edited by Jose Luis Gonzalez-Balado; *Suffering into Joy* (called simply "Suffering" below) (Servant Books, Ann Arbor, MI, 1996), written by Eileen and Kathleen Egan; to Penguin India for permission to reprint from *The Joy in Loving* (called simply "Joy" below) (Viking Penguin, New York, NY, original copyright 1996), compiled by Jaya Chaliha and Edward Le Joly; to Ballantine Books for permission to reprint from *A Simple Path* (called simply "Path" below) (Ballantine, New York, NY, 1995), compiled by Lucinda Vardey; to SPCK (the Society to Promote Christian Knowledge) for permission to reprint from the following two works: *Life in the Spirit* (simply called "Spirit" below) (Harper and Row, San Francisco, CA, 1983), edited by Kathryn Spink; *I Need Souls Like You* (called simply "Souls" below) (Harper and Row, San Francisco, CA, 1984), edited by Kathryn Spink; to HarperCollins and

HarperCollins United Kingdom for permission to reprint from the following five works: *My Life for the Poor* (called simply "Life" below) (Harper and Row, New York, NY, 1985), edited by Jose Luis Gonzalez-Balado and Janet N. Playfoot; *The Love of Christ: Spiritual Counsels, Mother Teresa of Calcutta* (called simply "Christ" below) (Harper and Row, San Francisco, CA, 1982), edited by Georges Corree and Jean Barbier; *A Gift for God: Mother Teresa of Calcutta* (called simply "Gift" below) (Harper and Row, New York, NY, 1975); *Mother Teresa: Her People and Her Work* (called simply "People" below) (Harper and Row, New York, NY, 1976), edited by Desmond Doig; *Mother Teresa of Calcutta: A Biography* (called simply "Calcutta" below) (Harper and Row, San Francisco, CA, 1983), by Edward Le Joly; to Liguori Publications and Jose Luis Gonzalez-Balado for permission to reprint from the following two works: *In My Own Words* (called simply "Words" below) (Liguori, Liguori, MO, 1996), compiled by Jose Luis Gonzalez-Balado (page numbers in the new Gramercy Books edition are noted with "GB" preceding); *Always the Poor* (called simply "Always" below) (Liguori, MO, 1980), edited by Jose Luis Gonzalez-Balado; to Ave Maria Press for permission to reprint from *Words to Love By* (called simply "Words" below) (Ave Maria Press, Notre Dame, IN, 1983), compiled by Frank J. Cunningham.

Other Sources

Love: A Fruit Always in Season, edited by Dorothy Hunt, (called simply "Fruit" below) (Ignatius Press, San Francisco, CA, 1987).

Works of Love Are Works of Peace: Mother Teresa of Calcutta and the Missionaries of Charity, edited with photographs by Michael Collopy (called simply "Works" below) (Ignatius Press, San Francisco, CA, 1996).

Mother Teresa by Navin Chawla (called simply "Mother" below) (Element Books, Rockport, ME, 1992).

Such a Vision of the Street by Eileen Egan (called simply "Vision" below) (Doubleday, New York, NY, 1985).

Further Acknowledgments

First let me simply offer sincere thanks for all the friends who helped. You know who you are.

Heartfelt gratitude to my original publisher Steven Scholl and the three literary agents involved at various stages—Kim Witherspoon, Gideon Weil, and Michele Rubin. I've also greatly appreciated the White Cloud Press team who has taken over where Steven left off: Stephen Sendar, Gary Kliewer, Christy Collins, and Raina Hassan. Their enthusiasm for this book has been a joy.

Many thanks are due all of my family, and especially my wife, Laura, and our three children Charles, Joe, and Marguerite, for bearing with the time this work has required of me.

A particular group in the publishing world did work absolutely crucial to my own—the editors and publishers of earlier compilations of Mother Teresa's wisdom, including Dorothy Hunt, Lucinda Vardey, Becky Benenate, Father Edward Le Joly, Bert Ghezzi, Jose Luis Gonzalez-Balado,

Kathryn Spink, Brother Angelo Devananda, Eileen Egan, Kathleen Egan, Joseph Durepos, Desmond Doig, and Jaya Chaliha. The first five in this group gave generously of their time to me directly, providing further assistance to make this book possible. Others in the publishing world who supported the project included Peter Edelman, Kris Kleimann, Amy Edelman, Paul Cash, and Marcia Broucek. Marcia also reminded me of the important gender issues involved with Mother Teresa's language.

Grateful thanks to Janet Murphy and all the staff at the Hastings-on-Hudson Public Library, for their endless inter-library loan efforts. Rowie Edelman and Debbie Boylan at the now defunct Good Yarns Bookstore also gave valuable assistance.

Thanks also to Sarah Sprague, Aaron Silverman, and Molly Maguire for their support of this book.

Finally, I'd like to express my deep gratitude to three people who are now all deceased. In my own pre-teen and teen years, they introduced me to the world of prayer: Annie Lee, Frank J. Bertino, and Rudi.

ABOUT THE AUTHORS

SAINT TERESA (1910-1997) was one of the most important religious figures of the twentieth century. She founded the Missionaries of Charity in Calcutta (Kolkata), India, was winner of the Noble Prize for Peace, and was described during her lifetime as "the most powerful woman in the world." She dedicated her life to serving "the poorest of the poor." She was canonized on September 4, 2016, and thereby recognized by the church as a saint. The anniversary of her death, September 5th, is her feast day.

DR. ANTHONY STERN attended Harvard College and Mount Sinai School of Medicine. He has worked in a variety of settings as a community psychiatrist, currently at a homeless shelter in Harlem, the Transitional Living Community of Weston United. He has written and given talks about the interface between religion and psychology over the last thirty years at diverse settings, including Sarah Lawrence College, the American Museum of Natural History, and the World Psychiatric Association.

Printed in the USA
CPSIA information can be obtained
at www.ICGtesting.com
JSHW080032041123
51447JS00002B/2